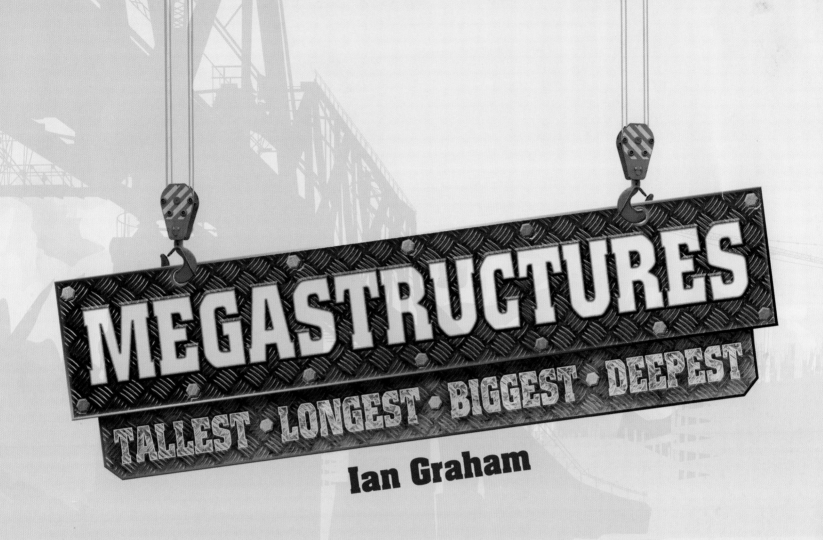

MEGASTRUCTURES

TALLEST · LONGEST · BIGGEST · DEEPEST

Ian Graham

FIREFLY BOOKS

A FIREFLY BOOK

Published by Firefly Books Ltd. 2012

Second printing, 2012

Publisher Cataloging-in-Publication Data (U.S.)

Graham, Ian, 1953–
    Megastructures : tallest longest biggest deepest / Ian Graham
[128] p. : ill. ; cm.
Includes index.
Summary: An in-depth look at the world's mightiest structures; why they were designed; how they were built, and how people use them.
ISBN-13: 978-1-77085-111-5 (pbk.)
1. Structural engineering – Miscellanea – Juvenile literature. I. Title.
624 dc23 TA634.G73 2012

Library and Archives Canada Cataloguing in Publication

Graham, Ian, 1953–
    Megastructures : tallest, longest, biggest, deepest / Ian Graham.
Includes index.
ISBN 978-1-77085-111-5
    1. Megastructures—Juvenile literature.
2. Building —Juvenile literature. I. Title.
NA9053.M43G73 2012   j720.4   C2012-902118-0

Published in the United States by
Firefly Books (U.S.) Inc.
P.O. Box 1338, Ellicott Station
Buffalo, New York 14205

Published in Canada by
Firefly Books Ltd.
66 Leek Crescent
Richmond Hill, Ontario L4B 1H1

Printed in China

This book was developed by:
QED Publishing
A Quarto Group company
226 City Road
London EC1V 2TT

Created for QED Publishing by Tall Tree Ltd www.talltreebooks.co.uk
Editor: Rob Colson
Designers: Malcolm Parchment and Jonathan Vipond
Illustrations: Apple Illustration and Caroline Watson

Picture credits
front cover: Philip Lange/Shutterstock
(t=top, b=bottom, l=left, r=right, c=center)
44-45 David Lee Photography; 45 Lee Jackson; 46 BLS AG; 56-57 Markuskun; 62-63 Femern AS Alamy: 8-9 Michael Doolittle/Alamy, 10 kpzfoto, 14 DBURKE, 39t Thomas Jackson; 46-47 qaphotos.com; 47 qaphotos.com; 53 Dominic Twist; 57 David R. Frazier Photolibrary, Inc. 67b Picture Contact BV, 89 Christine Osborne Pictures, 98t Doug Steley, 102t Danita Delimont, 107 Tom Tracy Photography, 110l QA Photos.com, 119l Ady Kerry; Andy Pernick 84b; Bill Ebbesen 109c; BP 116l; 116-117; Corbis 13t Joel W. Rogers, 13b Joel W. Rogers, 19 Sean Aidan, Eye Ubiquitous/CORBIS, 24-25 Jose Fuste Raga/CORBIS, 26-27 pix2go; 37b Mark Thiessen/National Geographic Society; 40 Imaginechina; 41t Frederic Stevens/epa; 62 Jacques Langevin/Sygma; 52-53 Andrew Kendrick/US Coast Guard; 54-55 Stringer/China/Reuters; 61 Bettmann; 62 Jacques Langevin/Sygma; 66 Xinhua Press, 66b Erich Schlegel, 69 Bettmann, 71 David Gray/Reuters, 77, Charles Lenars, 78 Danny Lehman, 87 Ed Kashi, 88t Jorge Ferrari/epa, 90t Andy Clark/X00056/Reuters, 90b Christopher Morris/VII, 93 Neil Tingle; 97b Paull A Souders, 100-101 Staff/Reuters, 103b Peter Andrews/Reuters, 104 Cezaro de Luca/epa, 105t Nadeem Khawer/epa, 110l Pascal Rossignol/Reuters, 110r Jacques Langevin/Sygma, 112-113 Najla Feanny, 112t Tom Fox/Dallas Morning News, 115r George Steinmetz, 118l Stefan Wermuth/Reuters; Creative Commons 21t Joi Ito, 24 Ratsbew, 25 Trubshaw, 29 Statoil; Dreamstime 12 Stuart Pearcey; Getty images 11 Science & Society Picture, 15, 39b Redeyed, 115l Natalia Bratslavsky; Eurotunnel 111t; Getty Images, 20t Bloomberg, 20b Barcroft Media, 21b AFP; 44 Cleland Rimmer/Fox Photos; 52b AFP; 58 Hulton Archive, 79t William West/AFP, 91 AFP, 97t Joe Raedle, 105b Hulton Archive, 111r AFP/Denis Charlet; Gump Stump 98-99; HKS 68; istockphoto 6-7 Mlenny Photography; Shutterstock 10-11 Shutterstock, 14-15 Cupertino, 16-17 WH Chow, 16 Jessmine, 17 Songquan Deng, 18 Henryk Sadura, 20-21 Philip Lange, 22-23 Elena Yakusheva, 22 Alexander Chaikin, 26 Rorem, 30-31, 101b Eduard Andras, 120-121 Robas; London 2012 80, 81; Markus Schweiss 102-103; NASA 86; NJR ZA 72b; Photolibrary 41b Thomas Frey, 99 The Print Collector; Populous 92; Risto Kaijaluoto 109; Shutterstock 96 Arnold John Labrentz, 106-107 Lee Prince, 113t Kola-Kola, 119r Natalia Bratslavsky; Shutterstock, 30 Bart J, 36-37 Jarno Gonzalez Zarraonandia; 37t Francisco Caravana 38-39 Laitr Keiows; 42-43 Manamana; 43t SVLuma; 43b clearviewstock; 48-49 Brendan Howard; 50-51 Antony McAulay; 51l E. Petersen; 55t Luis Santos; 58-59 Rafael Ramirez Lee; 59 Shutterstock; 60-61 r.nagy, 70 Caitlin Mirra, 72t prism68, 73 oksana. perkins, 74 Dudarev Mikhail, 75 Asier Villafranca, 75c Daniel M. Nagy, 76 Tom Cummins, 78 Gary718, 79b Chunni4691, 83 Joop Hoek, 84t Andy Z, 87 frontpage, 85 Elzbieta Sekowska, 88b Meewezen Photography; US Government 117t; Uploader 85

*Words in **bold** are explained in the Glossary on page 124.*

Contents

TOWERING GIANTS AND OTHER TALL MEGASTRUCTURES

Top 10 tallest skyscrapers

Skyscraper	Location	Height
Burj Khalifa	Dubai, UAE	2,717 feet (828 m)
Taipei 101	Taipei, Taiwan	1,667 feet (508 m)
Shanghai World Financial Center	Shanghai, China	1,614 feet (492 m)
International Commerce Center	Hong Kong, China	1,588 feet (484 m)
Petronas Towers	Kuala Lumpur, Malaysia	1,483 feet (452 m)
Greenland Financial Center	Nanjing, China	1,476 feet (450 m)
Willis Tower	Chicago, US	1,450 feet (442 m)
International Finance Center	Guangzhou, China	1,444 feet (440 m)
Jin Mao Tower	Shanghai, China	1,381 feet (421 m)
Two International Finance Center	Hong Kong, China	1,362 feet (415 m)

Aiming high

People have been fascinated by the construction of tall structures for thousands of years. Buildings that made everyone look skywards inspired awe and emphasized a ruler's wealth and power. Today, the tallest buildings are still expressions of wealth and power. They become famous and they make the places where they are built famous too.

Where are they built?

The tallest buildings are very expensive to construct, so they are usually built in the wealthiest parts of the world. For most of the 20th century, the world's tallest buildings were built only in North America. By the 1990s, countries such as Malaysia and Taiwan were building record-breaking skyscrapers. As China became wealthier in the 1990s and early 2000s, new skyscrapers were built in Chinese cities including Shanghai, Nanjing, Guangzhou and Shenzhen. Today, the astonishing 2,717 foot (828 m) Burj Khalifa in Dubai is the world's tallest skyscraper.

Why are they built?

Skyscrapers are built for practical reasons as well as for fame. Land in big cities is very expensive. By building upwards instead of spreading out across the ground, skyscrapers have a small **footprint**, but they pack a lot of homes, hotel rooms and offices into this small area. The tallest towers are useful in other ways too. They send radio and television signals over hills and tall buildings.

MEGA FACTS

The world's first skyscraper was the Home Insurance Building in Chicago, US. It was built in 1885 and was 10 stories high. It was demolished in 1931.

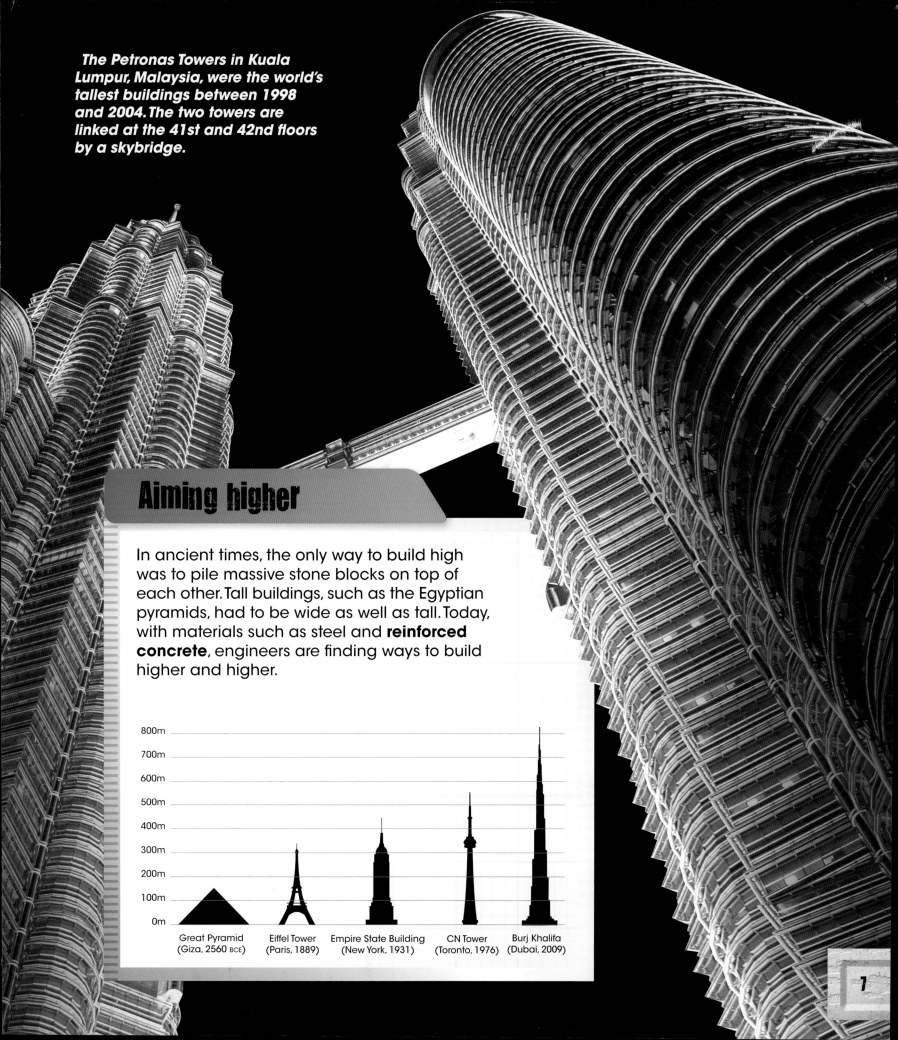

The Petronas Towers in Kuala Lumpur, Malaysia, were the world's tallest buildings between 1998 and 2004. The two towers are linked at the 41st and 42nd floors by a skybridge.

Aiming higher

In ancient times, the only way to build high was to pile massive stone blocks on top of each other. Tall buildings, such as the Egyptian pyramids, had to be wide as well as tall. Today, with materials such as steel and **reinforced concrete**, engineers are finding ways to build higher and higher.

800m
700m
600m
500m
400m
300m
200m
100m
0m

Great Pyramid
(Giza, 2560 BCE)

Eiffel Tower
(Paris, 1889)

Empire State Building
(New York, 1931)

CN Tower
(Toronto, 1976)

Burj Khalifa
(Dubai, 2009)

Superstructures

The part of a skyscraper or tower that is above the ground, called the **superstructure**, is supported by another part hidden under the ground, called the **substructure**. The substructure stops the building from sinking into the ground, and also helps to prevent the whole structure from falling over.

Supporting the weight

The weight of a house is held up by its walls. They are called **load-bearing walls**. If a skyscraper had load-bearing walls, they would have to be so thick that they would fill the base of the building. Instead, a skyscraper is held up by a frame that is usually made of steel. Thin walls, called **curtain walls**, hang from the building's frame like curtains.

The first skyscrapers

The 16-storey Monadnock Building in Chicago, US, was one of the world's first skyscrapers. The northern half of the building was built using load-bearing walls, which are nearly 7 feet (2m) thick at the base. The southern half of the building was built using a steel frame and curtain walls like a modern skyscraper. The thin curtain walls create more space inside, especially on the ground floor.

Inside a skyscraper there is a strong frame. It supports the building's weight so that the walls can be very thin.

Underground legs

A skyscraper or tower stands on a small base, like a pencil standing on end. A pencil falls over very easily, but skyscrapers and towers must not collapse. To prevent this from happening, they are anchored to concrete and steel legs, called **piles**, that extend deep underground. The piles rest on solid rock or on a concrete platform. This supports the building's weight and stops it from sinking. The piles also work like a tree's roots to hold the building upright. If the building tries to lean over, the ground grips the piles and holds it steady.

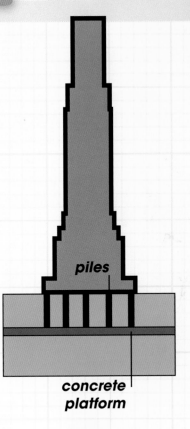

piles

concrete platform

Piles sit on the hard rock beneath the soil or on a specially constructed concrete platform.

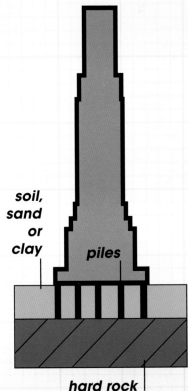

soil, sand or clay

piles

hard rock

MEGA FACTS

The Willis Tower in Chicago was the world's tallest skyscraper when it was completed in 1974. It is 1,450 feet (442 m) high and weighs 222,500 tons.

Standing up to nature

Once a skyscraper is built, it has to withstand everything that nature throws at it. It might face hurricane-strength winds or shaking caused by an earthquake. Engineers use models, test rigs and computer programs to ensure that wind and shaking will not cause problems.

The big blow

To withstand the pressure or pushing force of the wind, today's super-tall skyscrapers have to be 50 times stronger than a 197-foot (60 m) building of the 1940s. Model skyscrapers are placed in wind tunnels to study how the wind blows around them and to measure the wind pressure on the walls and windows. Computer models are used to show how the building bends and shakes, and to spot any weaknesses in the structure.

Wind tunnel testing

This model of a skyscraper and the buildings around it was built to be placed in a wind tunnel for testing. The model is on a turntable, which can be rotated to study the effects of wind blowing from different directions.

This massive ball is the 660-ton tuned mass damper in Taipei 101, a skyscraper in Taiwan.

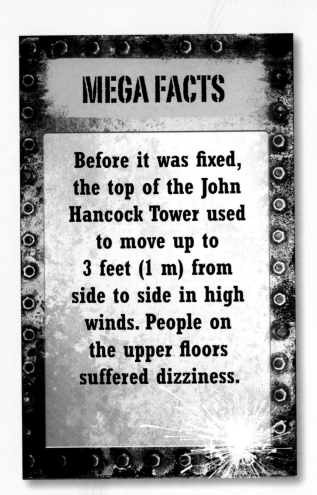

Shakin' all over

When the John Hancock Tower was built in Boston, US, in the 1970s, it swayed and twisted in the wind much more than expected. The swaying and twisting motions were happening in time with each other. This is called **resonance**, and it can make a building shake dangerously. One way to protect a building from resonance is to use a **tuned mass damper**. This is a heavy chunk of metal that can move from side to side. When the building sways in one direction, the damper moves in the opposite direction, tugging the building back and stopping it from swaying too much. Tuned mass dampers and 1,360 tons of steel beams, called braces, cured the John Hancock Tower's swaying.

Taipei 101's tuned mass damper hangs from the building's 92nd floor down to the 88th floor.

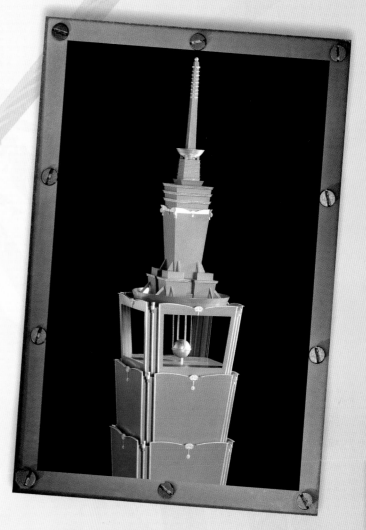

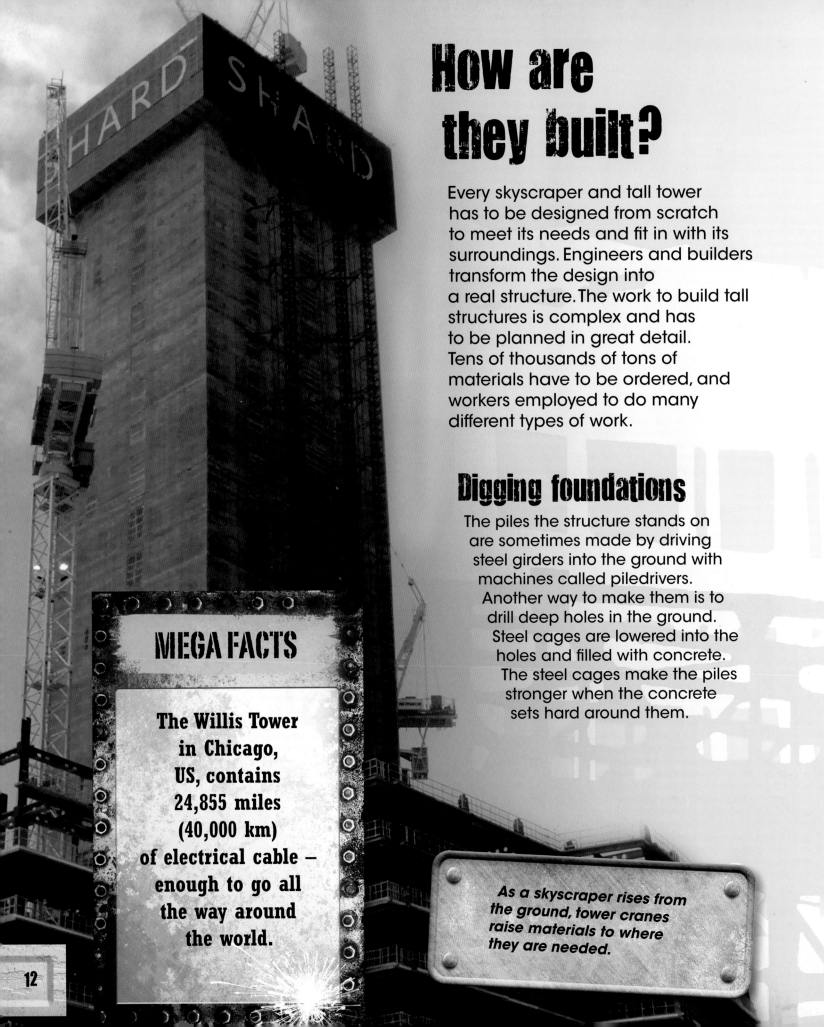

How are they built?

Every skyscraper and tall tower has to be designed from scratch to meet its needs and fit in with its surroundings. Engineers and builders transform the design into a real structure. The work to build tall structures is complex and has to be planned in great detail. Tens of thousands of tons of materials have to be ordered, and workers employed to do many different types of work.

Digging foundations

The piles the structure stands on are sometimes made by driving steel girders into the ground with machines called piledrivers. Another way to make them is to drill deep holes in the ground. Steel cages are lowered into the holes and filled with concrete. The steel cages make the piles stronger when the concrete sets hard around them.

MEGA FACTS

The Willis Tower in Chicago, US, contains 24,855 miles (40,000 km) of electrical cable – enough to go all the way around the world.

As a skyscraper rises from the ground, tower cranes raise materials to where they are needed.

Floors and walls

The floors are made by laying steel panels, called **decking**, between the beams. Concrete is poured on the decking to make the floors. The exterior wall panels are attached to the outside of the building's frame. A crane lifts them into position and workers bolt them in place.

Workers have laid out decking to make a floor in this skyscraper. Now they are pouring concrete on top and leveling it.

Framing up

The building's steel frame is built on top of the piles. The frames of older buildings, such as the Empire State Building in New York City, US, were held together using iron pins called **rivets**. Since the 1950s, skyscraper frames have been bolted or **welded** together.

Finishing touches

Once the frame has been completed, there is still a vast amount of work to be done. The electrical cabling, lighting, plumbing and air conditioning have to be installed. The interior walls and ceilings have to be fitted too.

A welder welds parts of a skyscraper's steel frame together. He wears a visor to protect his eyes from the bright flames.

Finishing touches

The building's steel frame was finished in September 2007 and the **cladding** was completed by June 2008. The Shanghai World Financial Center opened on August 28, 2008.

The cladding panels were lifted into position by two tower cranes.

Shanghai World Financial Center

In the 1990s, a new skyscraper was planned for Shanghai, China. The Shanghai World Financial Center was to be 1,509 feet high (460 m) making it the world's tallest building.

Construction began in 1997, but stopped due to a shortage of money. It started again six years later. The delay meant that by the time the building was finished, Taipei 101 in Taiwan had become the world's tallest building at 1,667 feet high (508 m). Plans were made to change the design of the Shanghai skyscraper so that it would be higher than Taipei 101, but the tallest it could go was 1,614 feet (492 m).

height: 1,614 feet (492 m)

The original design for the Shanghai World Financial Center was a tall, graceful, tapering tower with a circular hole at the top.

Changing shape

The hole near the top was originally designed to be round, but this was thought to look too much like the Japanese flag, so it was changed to an angular shape.

The Shanghai World Financial Center has 101 floors above ground and three floors below ground.

location: Shanghai, China

Famous giants

At the top, the Leaning Tower of Pisa leans nearly 13 feet (4 m) from the vertical.

There are thousands of skyscrapers, towers and other tall structures all over the world. Some of them are so distinctive that they are instantly recognizable. The Great Pyramid, the Leaning Tower of Pisa and the Empire State Building are among the world's most famous tall structures. Between them, they span 4,500 years of history.

The Great Pyramid

Built at Giza in Egypt in about 2560 BCE as a tomb for Pharaoh Khufu, the Great Pyramid was the world's tallest artificial structure for 4,000 years. It stands 479 feet high (146 m) and the base is 755 feet long (230 m) on each side. It was built from 2.3 million stone blocks weighing up to 13.6 tons each. It was originally clad in white limestone, but this was later stripped away and used to build other tombs or temples.

The Leaning Tower of Pisa

This famous leaning tower was built in Pisa, Italy, in the 12th century. It started sinking on one side, and leaning over, when it was only three floors high. Over the centuries, there were several attempts to stop it leaning further, but they all failed. Then in 1998, soil was removed from beneath the non-sinking side of the tower. This straightened up the tower a little and saved it from collapsing.

The Great Pyramid of Giza is the only one of the Seven Wonders of the Ancient World still standing.

The Empire State Building was built in New York City, US, in 1931. It was the first building to use the fast-track construction method that is commonly used today. To save time and cut costs, construction work began while the building was still being designed. It was built around a strong central core containing the elevator shafts. The outside of the building is covered with limestone and stainless steel. It was built in just 410 days, and at 1,250 feet high (381 m) excluding the spire, it was the tallest building in the world for 41 years.

The Empire State Building was designed with an airship terminal at the top. The plan was for passenger airships to tie up to the 203-foot (62 m) spire. However, strong winds blowing up the side of the building made it too dangerous so the terminal was cancelled.

spire

MEGA FACTS

From 1930 to 1931, three skyscrapers were built in New York City: first came 40 Wall Street, then the Chrysler Building, and finally the Empire State Building.

The observation deck is located on the 124th floor, about two-thirds of the way up. Two high-speed elevators carry visitors up to the deck in just three minutes.

Glass cladding

The superstructure is covered with a metal and glass cladding. Its 24,830 glass panels had to be cut to size by hand. The cladding has to be able to stand up to the extreme daytime heat and cooler nights of Dubai.

As it neared completion, the finishing touches were made to the cladding by workers in special moving platforms called gondolas.

location: Dubai, United Arab Emirates

Water supplies

A giant building needs an enormous amount of water for its occupants. Burj Khalifa's water system distributes 946,000 litres of water through the building each day. It comes from desalination plants that convert salty seawater into fresh drinking water.

Air conditioning

The tower is so tall that the temperature outside it is 13°F (7°C) lower at the top than at the base. This air is sucked into the building to help cool it, using a technique called "skysourcing".

By the time the cladding was added to the outside, Burj Khalifa was taller than two Empire State Buildings stacked on top of each other.

Mighty monuments

Monuments are structures built to remember people or events. They may be statues, columns, tombs, temples or other permanent structures. Two of the most instantly recognizable monuments are the Statue of Liberty in New York City, US, and the Eiffel Tower in Paris, France.

Just 240 visitors per day are allowed to climb the stairs to the Statue of Liberty's crown.

The Eiffel Tower

The Eiffel Tower was built as a monument to the French Revolution. It was completed in 1889. At a height of 1,024 feet (312 m), it was the world's tallest man-made structure. Today, communications **antennae** have raised its height to 1,063 feet (324 m). It was constructed from 18,038 pieces of iron. Its designer, Gustave Eiffel, was one of the first people to realize the importance of wind forces on tall structures. He designed the tower as an open lattice through which the wind could blow.

Paint protects the Eiffel Tower's iron structure from rusting. It is repainted every seven years. The job takes 25 painters more than a year and needs 60 tons of paint.

The Statue of Liberty

The Statue of Liberty stands on Liberty Island in New York Harbor. Before air travel, when people crossed the Atlantic Ocean by ship, it welcomed tourists and immigrants arriving in New York City. It was a gift to the US from France as a monument to freedom and democracy. With its stone base, it stands 305 feet high (93 m). It was made of copper sheets fixed to an iron tower. The tower was connected to the copper skin by an **armature** – a flexible framework that let the skin move in strong winds without cracking. The statue was built in France in 1884, then taken apart and shipped to New York. It was reassembled on the stone base in 1886.

By the 1980s, the armature supporting the Statue of Liberty's skin had corroded and needed to be replaced.

MEGA FACTS

The sunlit side of the Eiffel Tower expands more than the shaded side, making the top of the tower lean up to 7 inches (18 cm) away from the Sun.

Masts and towers

In past centuries, towers were built as defensive structures or to hold church bells high above the ground. Even taller towers are built today for long-distance communications. Radio signals have to be broadcast over long distances. This is done by transmitters on top of tall masts or towers.

Radio masts

Radio masts are usually made of an open lattice. The lattice is lighter than solid metal and it lets the wind blow through it. Unlike tall buildings, radio masts do not have any **foundations** under the ground to hold them upright. Instead, they are held up by cables called **guys** or metal rods called **stays** – just like the ropes that hold up tents.

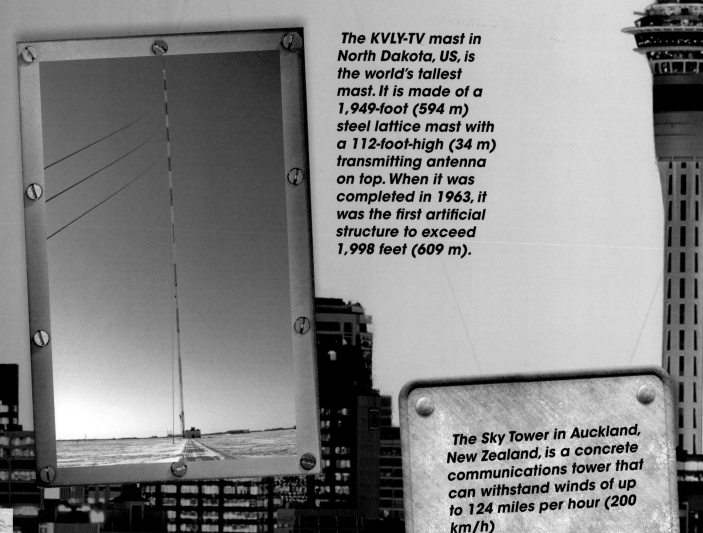

The KVLY-TV mast in North Dakota, US, is the world's tallest mast. It is made of a 1,949-foot (594 m) steel lattice mast with a 112-foot-high (34 m) transmitting antenna on top. When it was completed in 1963, it was the first artificial structure to exceed 1,998 feet (609 m).

The Sky Tower in Auckland, New Zealand, is a concrete communications tower that can withstand winds of up to 124 miles per hour (200 km/h)

Towers

Cities need radio antennae high above the ground because tall buildings often get in the way of radio and television signals. Radio masts may not be very pretty to look at, but they are usually located in remote places where their appearance does not matter. They are not suitable for use in cities because their guys and stays take up too much land. Sometimes, in cities, radio antennae are fixed to the tops of tall buildings, but if this is not possible, a communications tower is needed. Concrete towers are used because they look better than masts and they are self-supporting – they do not need guys or stays to hold them up.

Tourist attractions

Concrete communications towers often have observation decks and restaurants near the top. The 1,814-foot (553 m) CN Tower in Toronto, Canada, is the tallest concrete communications tower in the western hemisphere. At 1,076 feet (328 m), the Sky Tower in Auckland, New Zealand, is the tallest in the southern hemisphere. The world's tallest concrete communications tower is the Canton Tower in Guangzhou, China, which stands 2,001 feet (610 m) high. It was completed in 2010 in time to relay television pictures of the Asian Games. It is made of an open steel lattice wrapped around a strong concrete core.

The Canton Tower in Guangzhou, China, contains radio and television transmitters, observation decks, revolving restaurants, shops and cinemas.

MEGA FACTS

The KVLY-TV mast was built in 1963 in just 30 days. At 2,060 feet (628 m), it was the world's tallest artificial structure until Burj Khalifa was built.

The CN Tower

In the early 1970s, a number of skyscrapers were built in Toronto, Canada's biggest city. These new buildings made it difficult for people to receive radio and television programmes as they blocked the signal. The CN Tower was built in the middle of the city to broadcast signals from above the other buildings. It is one of the world's tallest towers. From the ground to the tip of its antenna, it stands 1,814 feet (553 m).

What a view!

The CN Tower opened to the public in 1976. Up to 2 million people visit it every year. They travel up the tower in lifts and visit two levels called pods near the top – the Main Pod and an even higher Sky Pod. The Main Pod has a revolving restaurant that makes a complete rotation every 72 minutes. There are also observation decks giving breathtaking views across the city. Brave visitors to one of the observation decks can stand on a glass floor and see the ground 1,122 feet (342 m) below their feet!

On a clear day, the view from the top of the CN Tower stretches to the horizon more than 100 miles (160 km) away.

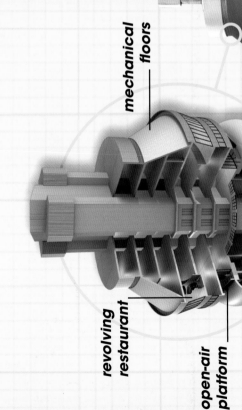

mechanical floors

revolving restaurant

open-air platform

microwave transmitter

`height: 1,814 feet (553 m)`

Finishing off

The concrete construction work was completed by March 1975. The 335-foot (102 m) steel antenna was lifted to the top in 44 pieces by a helicopter. The final section was bolted in place on April 2, 1975. The tower was opened to the public on June 26, 1976.

The tower's three-legged shape was produced by pouring concrete into a mold.

Building a giant

Construction work began in 1973. Most of the tower is made from concrete with a tall steel mast on the top. A six-sided pillar in the middle is surrounded by three massive supporting legs. The legs hold the tower steady in the strongest winds.

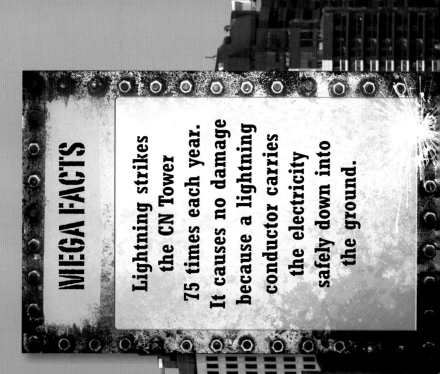

MEGA FACTS

Lightning strikes the CN Tower 75 times each year. It causes no damage because a lightning conductor carries the electricity safely down into the ground.

Offshore platforms

Offshore platforms stand in the sea and bring valuable oil and gas up from below the seabed. The part of an offshore platform that is above the waves is enormous, but the part that is under the sea is much, much bigger, and the whole structure is as tall as a skyscraper.

The tallest platforms are the ones that stand on the seabed on legs made of steel or concrete. Several decks of equipment and crew quarters, called the topsides, sit on top of the legs. The platform is towed out to sea and then tanks inside the legs are flooded so that they sink to the seabed. Only about 98 feet (30 m) of the legs are visible above the waves.

Offshore oil platforms are made on land and then towed out to sea.

EIRIK RAUDE

EIRIK RAUDE

EIRIK RAUDE
NASSAU

Record breaker

The biggest and heaviest structure ever transported is the Troll A gas platform. It stands in the sea about 50 miles (80 km) northwest of Bergen, Norway, bringing gas up from the Troll gas field. Its giant concrete legs are 1,211 feet (369 m) high and weigh an astonishing 656,000 tons. Troll A was built in the sheltered waters of a Norwegian **fjord**. When the legs were completed, they were partly submerged so that the decks could be lifted on top. Then the whole structure, now 1,549 feet (472 m) high, was towed out to its current position and sunk to the seabed. The massive legs buried themselves 115 feet (35 m) into the soft mud.

The Eiffel Tower was once the world's tallest man-made structure. The Troll A offshore platform is 525 feet (160 m) taller.

This oil platform is designed to drill in water depths of up to 9,843 feet (3,000 m).

Failures and accidents

Tall structures are designed to be safe and are built with great care, but sometimes something may go wrong. Although this is very rare, tall structures can suffer extraordinary accidents, failures and faults that their designers and builders had not anticipated. The tallest skyscrapers are covered with tens of thousands of windows. It is vital that they do not break or fall out. Large, heavy panels of glass falling from a skyscraper into the streets below could be lethal.

Falling windows

When the John Hancock Tower in Boston, US, was built in the 1970s, it was covered with blue, mirrored glass. Soon after the windows were installed, they started crashing to the ground. Researchers found that the **solder** (a metal **alloy**) that filled the space between the glass and frame was too stiff. When the panels flexed in the wind, as they were designed to do, the solder cracked. This cracked the glass and the windows fell out.

Dozens of radio masts have fallen down over the years. Most toppled in storms, while some were hit by aeroplanes. Others collapsed during maintenance work.

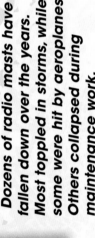

GIGANTIC LENGTHS AND OTHER VAST MEGASTRUCTURES

Top 10 Longest bridges and tunnels

Bridges	Location	Completed
Lake Pontchartrain Causeway	US	1956, 1969
Manchac Swamp Bridge	US	1970
Yangcun Bridge	China	2007
Hangzhou Bay Bridge	China	2007
Runyang Bridge	China	2005
Transport tunnels		
Seikan Tunnel	Japan	1988
Channel Tunnel	England-France	1994
Lötschberg Base Tunnel	Switzerland	2007
Guadarrama Railway Tunnel	Spain	2007
Iwate–Ichinohe Tunnel	Japan	2002

Over and under

Bridges and tunnels have been built since ancient times, but today they are bigger and longer than ever. These amazing engineering projects enable cars and other vehicles to take a more direct route across wide stretches of water or through the middle of mountains.

Building bridges

Bridges have developed from the simple ropes and vines that spanned rivers in prehistoric times to today's graceful steel and concrete structures that seem to defy gravity. The giant bridges built today are so long that they have to be shaped to fit the curve of the Earth's surface.

Tunnels

While bridges stand tall in the open for everyone to see, tunnels are hidden under the ground. The longest tunnels carry water into cities from distant **reservoirs**, but the most impressive tunnels are those through which we can travel: road and railway tunnels. The longest transport tunnel in use today is the Seikan Tunnel. This 34-mile (54 km) railway tunnel links the Japanese islands of Honshu and Hokkaido under the sea.

MEGA FACTS

The 85-mile-long (137 km) Delaware Aqueduct is the world's longest tunnel. It is part of a network that supplies New York City, US, with water.

The Bosphorus Bridge is a suspension bridge in Istanbul, Turkey. It links the continents of Europe and Asia.

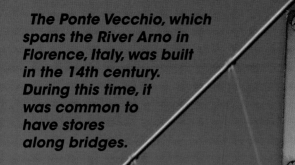

The Ponte Vecchio, which spans the River Arno in Florence, Italy, was built in the 14th century. During this time, it was common to have stores along bridges.

Particle smasher

There is a tunnel 574 feet (175 m) under the border between France and Switzerland that does not lead anywhere. It goes round in a circle, 17 miles (27 km) in circumference. The tunnel was built in the 1980s to house a scientific instrument called the Large Electron–Positron Collider. Subatomic particles were fired through a pipe inside the 12.5-foot-wide (3.8 m) tunnel, and scientists studied what happened when they collided. Today, there is a new scientific instrument, the Large Hadron Collider, in the tunnel.

Particles hurtle around the Large Hadron Collider at close to the speed of light.

The Akashi Kaikyo Bridge in Japan is strengthened by metal beams linked together in triangles, creating a very strong structure.

Building long

Bridge and tunnel designers and engineers have to overcome several problems. For example, bridges have to cope with every type of weather, from blistering heat to freezing cold. Tunnels have to resist the crushing weight of the ground above them.

Stretching bridges

Materials grow bigger when they heat up. On a hot day, a bridge expands and becomes longer. Joints, called expansion joints, are built into the **roadway** of a bridge. They let the roadway grow longer without causing any damage. Arch-shaped bridges made from steel **girders** expand in length and height when they heat up. Hinges are built into the arch to let it expand.

MEGA FACTS

On a hot day, the steel arch of Sydney Harbour Bridge can expand and rise by up to 7 inches (18 cm). Hinges at each end of the bridge let it rise and fall safely.

The Brooklyn Bridge

The Brooklyn Bridge links Brooklyn with Manhattan across New York City's East River. It was built between 1869 and 1883. The Brooklyn Bridge is a suspension bridge supported by two enormous **masonry** towers 1,594 feet (486 m) apart. When the bridge opened, it carried a pair of railway tracks with roads on each side and a **footpath** for pedestrians. The railway tracks were removed in 1944.

The Brooklyn Bridge was the first to have suspension cables made of steel. Until then, cables were made of iron.

Sydney Harbour Bridge

Australia's Sydney Harbour Bridge is the world's biggest steel arch bridge. The two halves of the arch were built out from opposite sides of the harbour until they met in the middle. Then the deck was hung from the arch. The whole bridge is held together by 6 million rivets, which were all driven into place by hand. The bridge carries eight vehicle lanes, two railway tracks, a footpath and a cycle lane.

The arch of the Sydney Harbour Bridge is 1,650 feet (503 m) long and rises to a height of 440 feet (134 m).

There had been plans for a bridge or tunnel across the estuary of the River Humber in northeast England, UK, since the 1870s, but work on the project did not finally begin until 1959. The first decision to be made was whether to build a bridge or a tunnel. A bridge was chosen because **geologists** found that the ground under the river was not suitable for tunneling.

Spanning the estuary

The shifting sands in the estuary meant that the deep-water channel used by ships kept moving. Because of this, the bridge could not rest on a series of piers across the river, so it was decided to build a suspension bridge. Construction work on the bridge began in 1973. A pier was built at each side of the river and a concrete tower was built on top of each pier. The towers are 4,626 feet (1,410 m) apart, and the total length of the bridge is 7,218 feet (2,200 m). The suspension cables were strung between massive concrete anchorages at each end of the bridge.

The bridge's towers are so tall that their tops sometimes peek out above the low clouds that settle over the river.

The supporting tower on the north bank of the river starts to take shape one year into the bridge's construction.

The Humber Bridge

length: 7,218 feet (2200 m)

When the Humber Bridge opened in 1981, it was the world's longest single-span suspension bridge. It held the record until 1998, when it was overtaken by Japan's Akashi Kaikyo Bridge.

Laying the deck

The deck was built in steel sections 72 feet (22 m) across – wide enough for four lanes of traffic. A 10-foot (3 m) strip added to each side of the deck carries cycle tracks and footpaths. The deck was hoisted into position, section by section, and hung from the cables. The bridge was completed in 1981.

MEGA FACTS

Because of the curvature of the Earth's surface, the Humber Bridge's towers are 1.5 inches (36 mm) further apart at the top than at the bottom.

The longest tunnels

Road and rail tunnels can cut hours off journey times by providing more direct routes through mountains. The longest tunnels include the Guadarrama Railway Tunnel in Spain and the Lötschberg Base Tunnel in Switzerland.

The train in Spain

In 2007, a new railway tunnel through the Guadarrama Mountains in Spain opened. The Guadarrama Railway Tunnel was Europe's fourth-longest rail tunnel. It was built to carry high-speed trains that run at up to 186 miles per hour (300 km/h). The twin-bore tunnel was carved out of the rock by four tunnel boring machines (TBMs). Two machines set out from the ends of the two tunnels towards each other. They were guided so accurately that they were only 4 inches (10 cm) out of line when they met. The TBMs bored two tunnels 31 feet (9.5 m) across. The two tunnels are connected every 820 feet (250 m) by cross-tunnels.

Through the Alps

The two tubes of the tunnel are connected to each other every 1,092.5 feet (333 m) so each tunnel can be used as an emergency escape route for the other tunnel.

The Alps mountain range forms a natural barrier between Italy and the rest of Europe. Since the 1870s, more than a dozen tunnels have been dug through the mountains. In 2007, the Lötschberg Base Tunnel opened, cutting the journey time between Germany and Italy by a third. The ground was very difficult to cut through because it was made of hard rock. Some of the tunnel could be dug by TBMs, but most of it had to be blasted out with explosives.

Falling ice

Cold weather can produce other dangers to traffic on a bridge. Ice can build up on the bridge's cables and **gantries** until chunks big enough to smash a car's windshield crash to the ground. Bridges may have to close if falling ice makes them too dangerous to cross.

Pinging cables

Some suspension bridges suffer from a problem that weakens their suspension cables. If moisture gets in between the steel wires that make up the massive cables, the wires rust. Within a few years, they start breaking. If this continues unchecked, year after year, the bridge will eventually become dangerously weak. Microphones attached to the cables pick up the pinging sounds made by the breaking wires. One way to stop the problem from getting any worse is to pump dry air through the cables to drive out the moisture. This process is called dehumidification.

The cables that hold up the Forth Road Bridge in Scotland, UK, wrap around holders, called yokes, in concrete chambers. The cables are regularly inspected for damage.

Monster spans

China's Hangzhou Bay Bridge and Portugal's Vasco da Gama Bridge are among the world's longest bridges. The Hangzhou Bay Bridge is the world's longest bridge over sea, while the Vasco da Gama Bridge is Europe's longest bridge.

China's record-breaker

The 22-mile-long (36 km) Hangzhou Bay Bridge links China's most populous city, Shanghai, with the city of Ningbo. The bridge crosses Hangzhou Bay, part of the East China Sea, an area with strong currents that is regularly battered by tropical storms. Most of the bridge is made of short spans sitting on top of piers anchored to the seabed, but two parts of the bridge are higher than the rest and are held up by cables hanging from towers. These cable-stayed spans have no supports below the deck, which means that ships can sail underneath them.

MEGA FACTS

Nearly 600 experts worked for nine years on the design of the Hangzhou Bay Bridge, because it was to be built in such a difficult place for a bridge.

The Hangzhou Bay Bridge carries a six-lane highway across the sea. It opened in 2008 and is designed to last for 100 years.

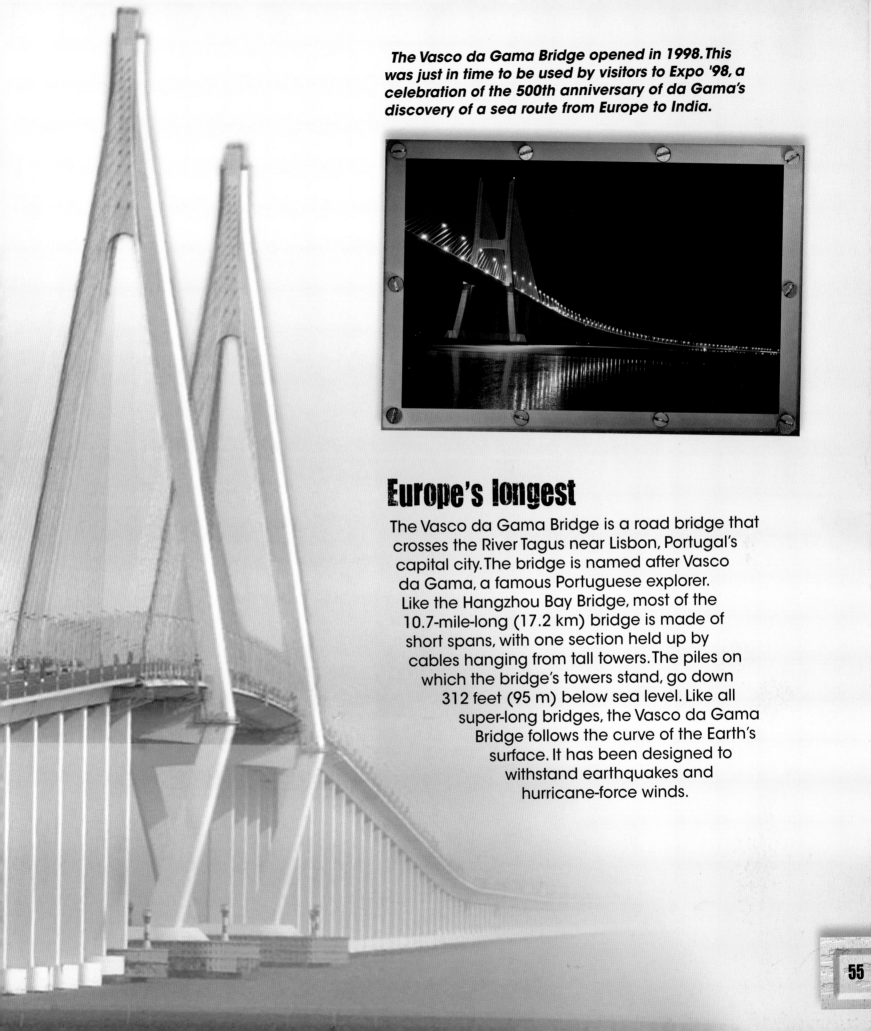

The Vasco da Gama Bridge opened in 1998. This was just in time to be used by visitors to Expo '98, a celebration of the 500th anniversary of da Gama's discovery of a sea route from Europe to India.

Europe's longest

The Vasco da Gama Bridge is a road bridge that crosses the River Tagus near Lisbon, Portugal's capital city. The bridge is named after Vasco da Gama, a famous Portuguese explorer. Like the Hangzhou Bay Bridge, most of the 10.7-mile-long (17.2 km) bridge is made of short spans, with one section held up by cables hanging from tall towers. The piles on which the bridge's towers stand, go down 312 feet (95 m) below sea level. Like all super-long bridges, the Vasco da Gama Bridge follows the curve of the Earth's surface. It has been designed to withstand earthquakes and hurricane-force winds.

The Lake Pontchartrain Causeway in Louisiana, US, is the world's longest bridge over water. From end to end, it measures 23.8 miles (38.4 km). It is so long that, because of the curved shape of the Earth's surface, someone standing at one end of the bridge cannot see the other end. The causeway spans Lake Pontchartrain, the second-biggest saltwater lake in the US. The city of New Orleans lies on the lake's south shore.

Twin bridges

The causeway is actually two bridges side by side. The first bridge was finished in 1956. It proved so popular that within 10 years, more than 3,000 vehicles were using it every day. A second bridge was built alongside. It opened in 1969. The bridges are linked together at seven points, so that traffic can cross from one bridge to the other in an emergency. There are also drawbridges, called **bascules**, that open to let boats through.

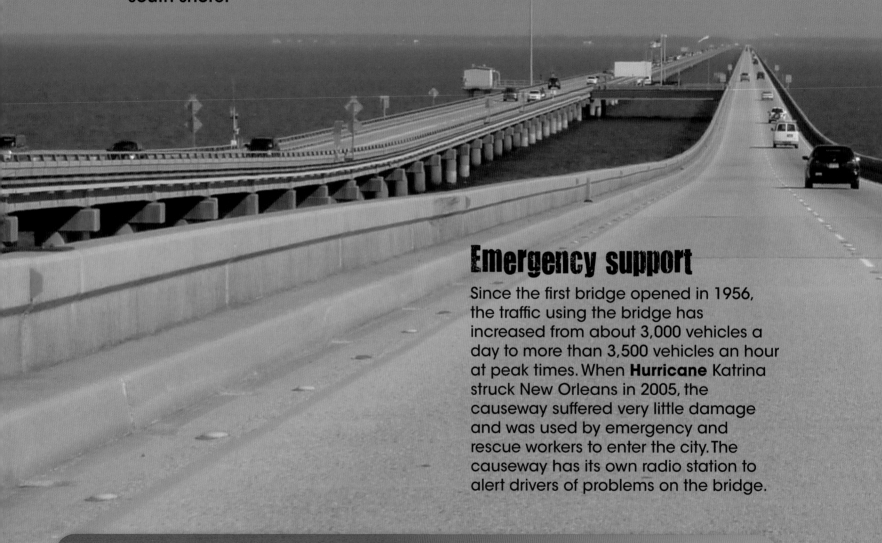

Emergency support

Since the first bridge opened in 1956, the traffic using the bridge has increased from about 3,000 vehicles a day to more than 3,500 vehicles an hour at peak times. When **Hurricane** Katrina struck New Orleans in 2005, the causeway suffered very little damage and was used by emergency and rescue workers to enter the city. The causeway has its own radio station to alert drivers of problems on the bridge.

Lake Pontchartrain Causeway

length: 23.8 miles (38.4 km)

A bascule opens to let boats through. Fenders protect the bridge from bumps by boats as they pass through. A radar system alerts officials if a boat comes within 1 mile (1.6 km) of the bridge.

The twin spans of the Lake Pontchartrain Causeway disappear over the horizon. Driving at 71.5 miles per hour (115 km/h), it takes more than 20 minutes to cross the bridge.

MEGA FACTS

The Lake Pontchartrain Causeway is so long that it spans one-thousandth of the Earth's circumference.

Subways

Railway systems that snake through a network of underground tunnels are called subways. They can move passengers across a busy city very quickly because the trains are not held up by heavy traffic or bad weather on the surface.

The first subway tunnels were built using the "cut and cover" method. First, a large trench was dug down the middle of a street. Then the street was rebuilt on top of the tunnel. Today, subway tunnels may be more than 197 feet (60 m) below the surface, and they are usually dug using tunnel boring machines (TBMs).

New York Subway

TBMs have become much more powerful over the years. The machine that is digging the new Second Avenue line in New York City, US, is as powerful as 12 jumbo jets and can grind its way through 59 feet (18 m) of rock a day. It was manufactured in about 1980 and has been used on at least four other projects. This latest subway line is due to open in 2016.

This tunnel boring machine was used during the construction of subway lines in New York City in the 1930s.

Going electric

London was the first city in the world to have an underground railway. The first section, the Metropolitan line, opened in 1863. Today, there are 11 lines with routes covering more than 249 miles (400 km). The Northern line is the deepest line: it is 230 feet (70 m) below ground in places. Electric trains were used from the beginning because they did not produce choking fumes like steam engines did.

Flooding is a problem in subway networks. More than 30 million litres of water a day are pumped out of the London Underground.

The subway system for San Francisco, known as the BART, has a WiFi system that allows passengers to access the Internet from the trains.

Failures and accidents

Engineers understand the forces that act on tunnels and bridges, but these enormous structures can sometimes surprise them. Accidents can happen to even the best designed structures. Bridge designers try to make their bridges flexible enough to soak up small movements caused by strong winds and traffic, but solid enough to stand safely for many years.

The wobbly bridge

When the Millennium Bridge, a footbridge across the River Thames in London, UK, opened in 2000, it swayed so much that it was nicknamed the "Wobbly Bridge." The problem was caused by something called synchronous lateral excitation. When people walked on the bridge, their footsteps made it sway a little from side to side. As soon as people felt this movement, they could not help walking in time with it, which made the swaying even worse. The bridge was closed while devices called dampers were fitted to fix the swaying.

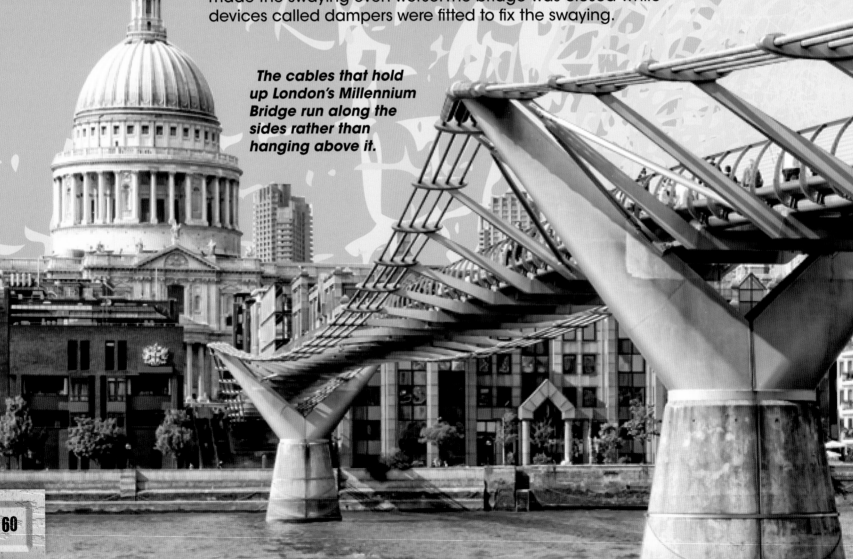

The cables that hold up London's Millennium Bridge run along the sides rather than hanging above it.

MEGA FACTS

In 1879, part of an iron railway bridge across the River Tay in Scotland collapsed in a storm. A passenger train crossing the bridge fell into the river.

Tunnel fires

Fires are a serious danger in tunnels. In 1999, a truck caught fire in the Mont Blanc Tunnel, which passes under Mont Blanc, Western Europe's highest mountain. The fire spread through the tunnel so fast that 39 people died. Over the next three years, shelters, fire-resistant wall coverings, smoke extractors, heat sensors and a fire station were built to make the tunnel safer.

Galloping Gertie

When a suspension bridge across the Tacoma Narrows Strait in Washington state, US, opened on July 1, 1940, it moved about so much in the wind that it was nicknamed "Galloping Gertie." Four months later, the bridge twisted back and forth so violently that it broke up. The collapse was caused by something called aeroelastic flutter. When the bridge started moving in the wind, its flexibility let it twist back and forth until it shook itself to pieces.

The roadway of the Tacoma Narrows Bridge hangs in shreds. A wind of only 40 miles per hour (64 km/h) made the bridge twist so much that it tore itself apart.

Future bridges and tunnels

The longest bridges and tunnels in use today are marvels of engineering, but even longer transport links are being planned. Some of these are bridges that will smash the records set by today's bridges. Many of the world's new bridges will be built in East Asia. In particular, China is now a wealthy country that wants to make it easier for businesses to move people, materials and products between its cities and ports.

Bering Bridge

One of the most daring plans is for a bridge to link Russia and the US across the Bering Strait. The bridge could carry a roadway, rail tracks and pipelines for oil and gas. Three bridges will be needed to span the strait – one from Russia to the Diomede Islands, one between the islands, and a third from the islands to Alaska, US. Two of the three bridges will have to be longer than China's Hangzhou Bay Bridge – the longest sea bridge in the world today.

A bridge across the Bering Strait would be 55 miles (88 km) long in total, passing over the Diomede Islands that lie halfway across the strait.

Crossing the River Pearl

The Hong Kong–Zhuhai–Macao Bridge in China will be 31 miles (50 km) long, with 22 miles (35 km) of it over the sea. This massive project includes an underwater tunnel, two artificial islands and a series of bridges. Today, it takes about three hours to cross the River Pearl from Zhuhai or Macao to Hong Kong. The new link will cut this to 30 minutes when it opens in 2016.

The Fehmarn Belt Bridge

By 2018, cars and trains may be able to travel from Denmark to Germany across a bridge or through a tunnel. The decision is due to be made in 2013. If a bridge is chosen, the 12-mile-long (20 km) link, called the Fehmarn Belt Bridge, will have a motorway and two railway tracks. Today, the journey takes about an hour by ferry, but with a bridge, the journey time would be slashed to 15 minutes.

The Fehmarn Belt Bridge will have two decks, one above the other. One will be for road traffic and the other for trains.

MEGA FACTS

A bridge across the Bering Strait would stand on 220 piers built in icy water and strengthened to protect them from the impact of icebergs.

MASSIVE MONSTERS AND OTHER HUGE MEGASTRUCTURES

Top 10 biggest stadiums by capacity

Stadium	Location	Capacity
May Day Stadium	Pyongyang, North Korea	150,000
Salt Lake Stadium	Kolkata, India	120,000
Aztec Stadium	Mexico City, Mexico	115,000
Michigan Stadium	Michigan, US	109,901
Beaver Stadium	Pennsylvania, US	107,283
Neyland Stadium	Tennessee, US	102,455
Ohio Stadium	Ohio, US	102,329
Bryant–Denny Stadium	Alabama, US	101,821
Darrell K Royal Stadium	Texas, US	100,119

Building big

People have been building massive structures for thousands of years. The biggest structures built today include dams and artificial islands. The most familiar giant structures are sports **stadiums**, which are built in cities where millions of people can see and visit them.

Holding water

Dams are barriers built across rivers and other bodies of water. When a river is blocked by a dam, the water rises behind it to form a large lake called a reservoir. The water pushes against the dam with a huge force, so dams have to be heavy and strong to hold back the water. A reservoir supplies fresh water to the surrounding region. Large dams also work as power stations. Water from the reservoir flows through turbines inside the dam. This makes the turbines spin, driving **generators** that produce **hydroelectricity**.

MEGA FACTS

The world's biggest sports stadium is the May Day Stadium in Pyongyang, the capital city of North Korea. It can hold 150,000 spectators.

The Cowboys Stadium, home of Dallas Cowboys American Football team, in Arlington, Texas, is the biggest domed stadium. It opened in 2009 and can seat 80,000 spectators.

Building strength

The Bird's Nest Stadium was designed to withstand earthquakes.

The Bird's Nest Stadium in Beijing, China, is made of a network of steel beams. It reached its full strength only when it was complete. The stadium was supported by 78 temporary columns while it was being built. When it was completed, the columns were removed.

Building methods

How a building is constructed depends on the type of structure. A concrete dam is built by pouring concrete into a mold. Concrete is very strong in compression (when it is squeezed), but it cracks easily when it is bent or stretched. To strengthen the concrete, it is poured over steel rods called reinforcing bars, or rebars. The concrete sets hard around them. This is called reinforced concrete.

Foundations

Some structures are so big and heavy that their weight is enough to keep them in position. The biggest and heaviest dams work like this. But most structures have to be anchored securely to the ground so that they do not move, sag or twist. They stand on underground pillars called piles. The piles provide a firm foundation for the building.

MEGA FACTS

China's Bird's Nest Stadium was built from 7,500 steel beams. No two beams were alike. Each one was designed separately to ensure that they all fitted together.

Famous giants

The biggest structures of the Ancient World were pyramids, stadiums, tombs and temples. The heaviest and most impressive of all was the Great Pyramid of Khufu. The Colosseum in Rome was probably the world's first great stadium, and could hold 50,000 spectators. Today, the biggest structure of all is an airport terminal.

The biggest pyramids

The Great Pyramid of Khufu was built as a tomb for the Egyptian Pharaoh Khufu around 4,500 years ago. It weighs nearly 6 million tons and is the heaviest man-made structure on Earth, but it is not the biggest. The Great Pyramid of Cholula in Mexico is bigger. Today, it looks like a natural hill, but it was once a giant stone pyramid.

The Great Pyramid of Khufu (above right) is one of a trio of pyramids built at Giza, Egypt.

The Colosseum's arena measures 249 feet (76 m) by 144 feet (44 m) – about half the size of a soccer field. Its wood and stone floor was covered with sand.

The Colosseum

The Colosseum was the Roman Empire's biggest **amphitheatre**, built to entertain people. The entertainment was often violent, including public executions and fights between gladiators. The Colosseum was constructed more than 1,900 years ago. It is an oval building, 617 feet (188 m) long, 512 feet (156 m) wide and 159 feet (48.5) high. It was built from limestone, bricks, concrete and volcanic rock.

Terminal 3 at Dubai International Airport covers the same area as 280 soccer fields.

Modern marvel

In terms of floor space, the biggest building today is Terminal 3 of Dubai International Airport, UAE. It has 16.2 million square feet (1.5 million m²) of floor space, and was built from enough concrete to fill 950 Olympic-size swimming pools. The concrete was reinforced by 450,000 tons of steel and a further 33,000 tons of steel were used to build the supporting structure.

MEGA FACTS

For 3,800 years, the Great Pyramid of Khufu, at 456 feet (139 m) high, was the tallest building in the world. The record was taken from it in 1311 by Lincoln Cathedral, UK.

Sydney Opera House stands on a plot of land jutting out into Sydney Harbour, surrounded on three sides by water. It was designed by the Danish architect Jørn Utzon, who won a competition in the 1950s to find the best design. Utzon's winning design resembled a set of curved shells nestling inside each other.

Running late

Construction of the Opera House began in 1959, and was expected to take about four years. However, its unique shape posed a series of tricky engineering problems. It finally opened 10 years late and 14 times over budget.

The Opera House appears to float on the waters of Sydney Harbour. The area it covers is big enough to park four jumbo jets.

Sydney Opera House

year completed: 1973   length: 607 feet (185 m)

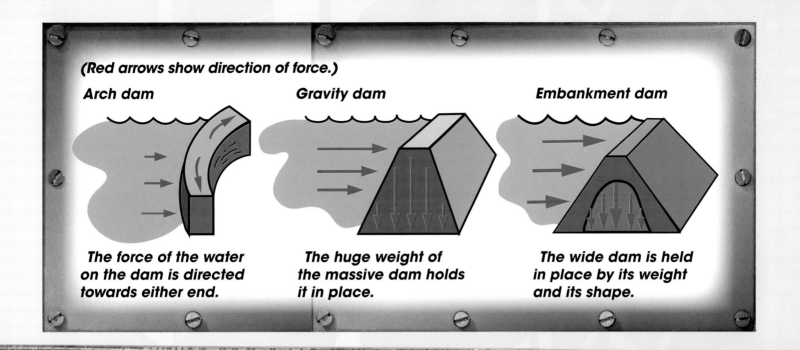

(Red arrows show direction of force.)

Arch dam

The force of the water on the dam is directed towards either end.

Gravity dam

The huge weight of the massive dam holds it in place.

Embankment dam

The wide dam is held in place by its weight and its shape.

Afsluitdijk

One of the most ambitious dams ever built is the Afsluitdijk in the Netherlands. It is an embankment dam, and spans the mouth of the Zuiderzee, an inlet of the North Sea. The Afsluitdijk changed part of the Zuiderzee to a vast freshwater lake, called the IJsselmeer.

The Afsluitdijk was built between 1927 and 1933. It is 20 miles (32 km) long and 295 feet (90 m) wide.

In the 1920s, the US government decided to build a dam across the Colorado River on the border of Arizona and Nevada. It was to be a massive, concrete arch-gravity dam.

Diverting the river

First, the course of the Colorado River had to be changed so that it flowed around the part of the river bed where the dam was to be built. This was done by blasting four tunnels through the walls of the Black Canyon.

The first concrete was poured in June 1933. The dam could not be made in one seamless block, because the concrete would have cracked as it set. Instead, the concrete was poured into molds that formed blocks up to 161 square feet (15 m²) and 5 feet (1.5 m) high. The blocks contained pipes. Chilled water was pumped through the pipes to make the concrete set more slowly and evenly to avoid cracking. Then the pipes were filled with **grout**. The vast concrete wall of the dam was finished in May 1935.

MEGA FACTS

The Hoover Dam contains enough concrete to make a two-lane highway from San Francisco to New York — a distance of 2,564 miles (4,126 km).

The curved wall of the Hoover Dam seen here before Lake Mead had been created. The whole dam weighs nearly 6 million tons.

The Hoover Dam

length: 1,243 feet (379 m)   height: 659 feet (201 m)

Powerhouse

The last part of the dam to be built was the **powerhouse**, where electricity would be generated. The tunnels were blocked, so the Colorado River followed its natural course again. A new lake called Lake Mead filled up behind the dam. When the water was deep enough, it entered four tall intake towers and flowed through the turbines. The spinning turbines powered the electricity generators.

A row of huge turbines spin in the powerhouse.

Mega workplaces

The biggest buildings on Earth are not cathedrals, monuments or sports stadiums. They are workplaces, such as factories and office buildings. The world's largest planes are built in massive buildings. The Pentagon, a US government office building, is the world's biggest office building.

Building spacecraft

The Vehicle Assembly Building (VAB) in Florida, US, is the world's largest single-storey building, at 525 feet (160 m) high, 715 feet (218 m) long and 518 feet (158 m) wide. It was built at the Kennedy Space Center in the 1960s to assemble the Saturn V rocket, which was used to launch the Apollo space missions. Its giant overhead cranes can lift rockets and spacecraft weighing up to 227 tons.

The Kennedy Space Center's VAB has the world's biggest doors. Each of the four doors is 456 feet (139 m) high.

Mega factory

Boeing's airliner factory in Everett, Washington State, US, is the largest building in the world by volume (the amount of space inside it). It is more than twice the size of the next biggest – the factory in France that builds the world's biggest airliner, the Airbus A380. The Everett plant covers 470 million cubic feet (13.3 million m³) – the whole of Disneyland could fit inside with room to spare.

Thirty thousand people work at Boeing's Everett assembly plant, the biggest factory in the world.

The Pentagon

The Pentagon, headquarters of the US Department of Defense, is the world's biggest office building by floor area (6.5 million square feet/604,000 m²). About 23,000 people work in the Pentagon, so named because of its five-sided shape. It has five floors above ground level and another two below ground.

It was built during World War II (1939–45). Steel was in short supply then, so the Pentagon's concrete structure was reinforced with as little steel as possible.

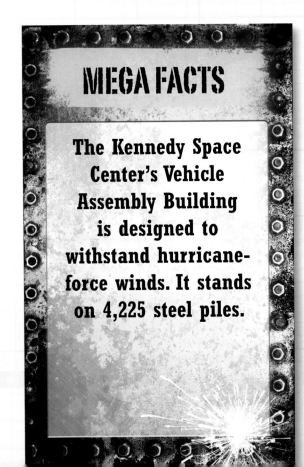

Because of its shape, it takes no more than seven minutes to walk between any two offices in the Pentagon.

MEGA FACTS

The Kennedy Space Center's Vehicle Assembly Building is designed to withstand hurricane-force winds. It stands on 4,225 steel piles.

Artificial islands

People started making artificial islands thousands of years ago in the Stone Age. Small islands were constructed by piling up rock and earth in shallow water. Compared to the hand-built islands of past times, today's artificial islands are monsters. They are built to provide new land for homes, hotels and airports.

The artificial Palm Islands in Dubai, UAE, are made of sand. A circular breakwater, made of rock, protects them from the waves.

Polders

The Dutch are the masters of reclaiming land from the sea and lakes. The area to be reclaimed is enclosed by building an embankment called a dyke. Then the water is pumped out to leave dry land. Land reclaimed like this is called a polder. The Dutch have created more than 3,000 polders in the past 1,000 years.

The new land created by polders is very flat. With no hills to break the wind, they are ideal for windmills.

Multi-purpose stadiums

Many stadiums built today are usually designed for one sport only – such as football, baseball or track and field. Future stadiums will be able to change their playing surface more easily so that different sports can be played. The lowest layer of seats might be able to slide back to reveal a running track. A grass soccer field can be built in sections and these might be slid outside to reveal a hard surface for pop concerts or even motor sports.

The 40,000-seat Olympic Stadium in Sochi, Russia, will host the opening and closing ceremonies of the 2014 Winter Olympics. Soccer matches will be held there during the 2018 World Cup.

The "IT" factor

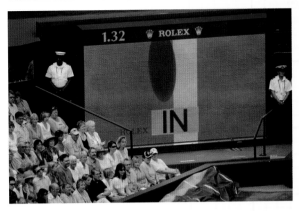

At major tennis events such as Wimbledon large screens show computer-generated replays.

Future stadiums will be wired for information technology (IT). Spectators will be able to watch the action on screens all over the stadium. They will also be able to download information and video clips to mobile telephones.

DARKEST DEPTHS AND OTHER UNDERGROUND MEGASTRUCTURES

10 of the world's deepest digs and bores

Type of dig/bore	Name	Location/Depth
Deepest borehole	Kola Superdeep Borehole	Russia/40,230 feet (12,262)
Deepest oil well	Tiber oil well	Gulf of Mexico/35,049 feet (10,683 m)
Deepest mine	TauTona gold mine	South Africa/12,795 (3,900 m)
Deepest European metal mine	Pyhäsalmi mine	Finland/4,724 feet (1,440 m)
Deepest open-cast mine	Bingham Canyon mine	US/3,937 feet (1,200 m)
Deepest diamond mine	Wesselton mine	South Africa/3,264 feet (995 m)
Deepest undersea tunnel	Eiksund Tunnel	Norway/942 feet (287 m)
Deepest rail tunnel	Seikan Tunnel	Japan/787 feet (240 m)
Deepest hand-dug hole	The Big Hole diamond mine	South Africa/705 feet (215 m)
Deepest subway tunnel	Pyongyang Metro	North Korea/361 feet (110 m)

Digging down

Deep holes are dug in the ground to get at fossil fuels such as coal and oil. Deep tunnels may be excavated to safely dispose of dangerous materials such as the **radioactive** waste from nuclear power stations. Tunnels also allow cars or trains to travel underneath mountains or seas.

Mining

Mines are dug to bring valuable and useful materials up from deep underground. Most of these materials are part of the rock itself. Rock is made of **minerals**, and some minerals contain the metals and other substances that we want to use. These minerals are called ores. Mines are dug down to reach the rock that contains the valuable ores.

MEGA FACTS

As long as 2,000 years ago, the Chinese drilled holes in the ground to reach water. They used bamboo drill pipes fitted with iron cutting bits at the end.

Drilling

Coal and minerals have to be cut out of the ground, but oil and gas will come to the surface by themselves. If a hole is drilled down to oil and gas trapped underground, the pressure will squirt them all the way up to the surface. Scientists drill holes in the ground to bring up samples of earth, rock and ice for research. Water pumped down drill-holes can be heated by hot rocks deep underground. When the hot water comes back up to the surface, the heat can be used to warm buildings or to make electricity.

Oil workers connect a pipe to the drill in order to collect oil that is forced to the surface from deep underground.

Tunneling

Deep tunnels allow cars and trains to pass underneath mountains, rivers and even the sea. Deep tunnels are also used to store dangerous substances. Nuclear reactors produce waste that cannot be thrown away like ordinary garbage because it is radioactive. This means that it gives out dangerous rays and particles. One way to deal with it is to store it in deep tunnels. The Waste Isolation Pilot Plant in New Mexico, US, stores radioactive waste in underground tunnels 2,133 feet (650 m) below the surface.

Drums full of radioactive waste arrive at the bottom of a shaft 2,133 feet (650 m) underground in the Waste Isolation Pilot Plant in New Mexico.

The tunnels in mines are big enough for mechanical diggers, drilling machines and even trains to fit inside.

Deep challenges

The immense pressure deep underground creates a lot of difficulties for deep digging or drilling. Rock can fly out of a mine's walls, oil and gas can erupt from a well like lava from a volcano, and tunnels can cave in as they are being dug.

In April 2010, an underwater blow-out caused the Deepwater Horizon oil rig in the Gulf of Mexico to explode.

Rock burst

Rock at great depths underground is squashed by the weight of all the ground above it. When a deep mine is dug, the huge weight pressing down on it can make rock explode out of its walls. Called **rock burst**, it is a great danger in the world's deepest mines.

In deep mines, rock that looks dangerous, perhaps because it is cracked, can be covered with steel mesh or blown out with explosives before it bursts.

Blow-outs

Oil and gas trapped deep underground are under tremendous pressure. When an **oil well** is drilled, the oil or gas cannot be allowed to gush out of the top of the well. A safety valve called a **blow-out** preventer is fitted to the top of a well. If oil or gas tries to gush out – an emergency called a blow-out – the blow-out preventer seals the well.

Going superdeep

In the 1970s, scientists in the Soviet Union drilled the deepest hole in the **Earth's crust**. The Kola Superdeep Borehole is 40,230 feet (12,262 m) deep. Drilling was stopped in 1992 because the rock at the bottom was too hot. It was 356°F (180°C) – nearly twice as hot as boiling water. Had they continued drilling down to the target of 49,213 feet (15,00 m), scientists calculated that the temperature would have reached 572°F (300°C)!

A special commerative stamp was released in 1987 to celebrate the digging of the Kola Superdeep Borehole.

The Holland Tunnel

In the early 1900s, ferries crossing the Hudson River between New York and New Jersey were carrying 30 million vehicles a year. It was clear that a permanent link was needed to carry this traffic, so the Holland Tunnel was built. Tests revealed that the carbon monoxide gas given off by car engines was lethal, so fresh air had to be pumped in to clear out the dangerous fumes. The tunnel opened in 1927 and is still in use today.

Drilling

The oil and natural gas that fuel the modern world is formed deep underground. They are brought up to the surface by drilling holes in the ground. Scientists drill deep holes in the ground too, to learn more about the Earth and its past.

Oil and gas are found by looking for the right kind of rocks in the ground. Geologists search for two types of rock, called reservoir rocks and cap rocks. Reservoir rocks are porous, which means that they have holes in them. The oil and gas fill the holes, like a sponge full of water. The right kind of rock must also form above the oil and gas to prevent them from bubbling up to the surface. This cap rock traps the oil and gas underground. When oil and gas are found, a hole is drilled down to them by a metal pipe with a toothed drill bit at the end. The drill is held by a tower called a **derrick**. Once the drilling rig strikes oil or gas, the top of the well is fitted with a series of valves to control the flow of oil or gas.

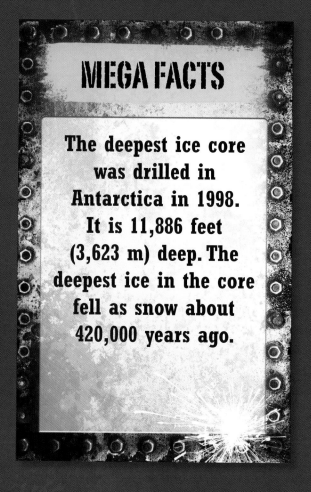

MEGA FACTS

The deepest ice core was drilled in Antarctica in 1998. It is 11,886 feet (3,623 m) deep. The deepest ice in the core fell as snow about 420,000 years ago.

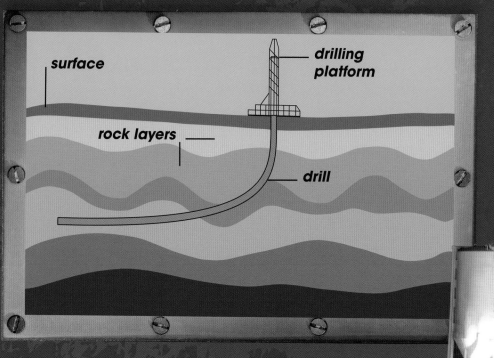

surface

drilling platform

rock layers

drill

Drills do not have to go straight down. The end of a drill can be steered. This is called directional drilling. It is used when a drilling platform cannot be placed directly above an oil or gas field.

engine

Ice cores

Holes are drilled through ice with a hollow drill-pipe. When the drill is pulled up, the ice inside the pipe, called an **ice core**, comes up with it. The ice was once snow that fell on the ground. The weight of new snow on top squashed the snow underneath and changed it to solid ice. The deeper the ice, the older it is.

Scientists study ice cores to learn about the climate in the past. The thickness of the layers of ice in the core shows how much it snowed every year. Little bits of plants, particles of soot or ash and even bubbles of ancient air trapped in the ice give more clues.

These scientists are drilling an ice core on a mountain-top in Bolivia. The drill is powered by electricity made by solar panels.

derrick

turntable

Inside the derrick, a turntable turns the pipe. The pipe turns a tough cutter called a drill bit.

Thunder Horse is an **oil field** in the Gulf of Mexico. It was discovered in 1999 by a drillship called *Discoverer 534,* and is one of the deepest oil fields ever found.

Drillships search for oil by drilling holes called exploration wells. *Discoverer 534* lowered its drill to the seabed and drilled down 25,755 feet (7,850 m) before it struck oil. Another drillship, the *Discoverer Enterprise,* drilled a second exploration well and also struck oil. A production platform was brought in to extract the oil. The production platform is called the Thunder Horse PDQ (production drilling quarters). It is a giant structure in which up to 229 people can live and work.

Flame boom

Derrick

Crane

Towing tug

The Discoverer Enterprise *drilled one of the first wells in the Thunder Horse oil field.*

Thunder Horse Oil Field

water depth: 6,050 feet (1,844 m)

Hurricane damage

Thunder Horse was due to begin producing oil and gas in 2005. However, the workers had to be taken off the rig because a hurricane was heading for it. When they returned, they found the platform leaning over at an angle. It was repaired quickly, but then cracks were found in pipes at the top of the well on the seabed. As a result, Thunder Horse began producing oil and gas only in 2008.

Living quarters

Lifeboats

The Thunder Horse PDQ was tipped over in July 2005 by Hurricane Dennis.

Supporting leg

The Thunder Horse PDQ is built on top of four massive legs that stand on a hull just under the surface of the water.

MEGA FACTS

The Thunder Horse production platform produces enough oil to power the homes of 80,000 people.

Deep dangers

Deep mines and drill-holes can sometimes damage the land around them. Tunnels can cause problems for the vehicles that travel through them. Compared to the countless trillions of tons of rock and earth all around them, mines and drill-holes are tiny pinpricks in the Earth's crust. Even so, they can upset the delicate balance of underground forces.

Making quakes

Deep mines can change underground forces just enough to trigger an earthquake. A geothermal power plant in Basel, Switzerland, was closed down in 2009. It was believed to have triggered an earthquake under the city three years earlier.

Coal mining may have triggered the biggest earthquake in Australia's history in Newcastle, New South Wales, in 1989.

Work was stopped at the Deep Heat Mining geothermal experiment in Basel, after injections of high-pressure water triggered a small earthquake.

In freezing cold weather, the heat inside a long, deep tunnel, such as the Channel Tunnel, can melt snow on a train.

The wrong kind of snow

Trains ground to a halt in the Channel Tunnel on December 18, 2009 due to cold temperatures outside the tunnel. Snow was blowing against the trains as they headed towards the French end of the tunnel. The power cars at the front and back of each train have ventilation grills on each side to let in air for cooling. A sheet of material behind the grill normally stops snow from getting through, but the snow on that night was so powdery that it got in. The warm air in the tunnel melted the snow, and the water ran into the electronic systems, which then broke down.

MEGA FACTS

More than 200 earthquakes since the 1940s in the US may have been caused by mining, drilling and other human activities.

Digging deep holes in the ground, such as this old mine in Alaska, US, is thought to trigger earthquakes, even in places where earthquakes are rare.

Underground power

Holes drilled in the ground can be used to make electricity. The power stations that do this are called geothermal power stations. They make electricity using heat from deep underground, where volcanic activity can turn water into super-hot steam.

Drilling for heat

To use the heat, holes are drilled at least 1.8 miles (3 km) deep into the ground. Cold water is pumped down some of the drill-holes. Deep underground, the water soaks up heat from hot rock. If the rock is hot enough, the water changes into steam. The hot water or steam comes back up to the surface through more drill-holes. The heat can be used to heat buildings or to make electricity.

MEGA FACTS

The first geothermal power station was built in Larderello, Italy, in 1904. Today, there are geothermal power stations in 24 countries.

This geothermal power station in Iceland empties hot water into a nearby lagoon, where people bathe in waters that are at least 99°F (37°C) all year round.

Power stations

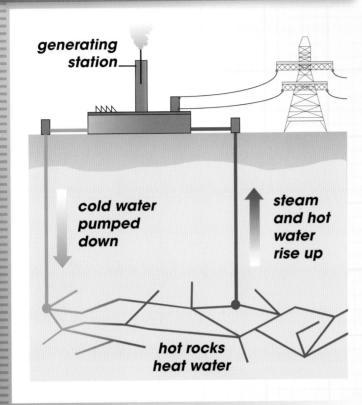

generating station

cold water pumped down

steam and hot water rise up

hot rocks heat water

To make electricity, steam coming up out of the drill-holes makes drums, or wheels called turbines, spin very fast. The spinning turbines power generators, which make electricity. If there is not enough heat underground to make steam, the hot water is used to heat a different liquid that turns to a gas at a lower temperature than water.

Geothermal power stations pump cold water into hot rocks deep underground.

The Geysers

The biggest group of geothermal power stations in the world is in California, US, at a place called The Geysers. More than 350 wells have been drilled down to a depth of 2 miles (3.2 km). Water pumped underground comes back to the surface as steam for making electricity. After the steam has been used, it is not wasted.

The steam is cooled to change it back to water, which is sent underground again to make more steam and more electricity. The 22 geothermal power stations at The Geysers produce enough electricity for more than 1 million people.

Future digs

The undersea tunnels, deep mines and drill-holes that have been made in the Earth's crust are very ambitious projects, but there are even more amazing projects to come in the future. There are plans for undersea tunnels to join Japan and Korea, Europe and Africa, and the US and Russia. Some future transport links, such as the new Hong Kong–Zhuhai–Macau link, will combine bridges with tunnels.

In the future, cars could drive through underwater tunnels held in place by tethers attached to floating pontoons.

MEGA FACTS

The US and Russia could be linked by a tunnel under the Bering Strait. Called the TKM-World Link, it would be about 62 miles (100 km) long.

New tunnel projects

A tunnel could be built to link Japan and Korea. At 124 miles (200 km) long, it would be the longest ever transport tunnel. The narrow sea channel between Spain and Morocco could be crossed by a tunnel. Linking Europe and Africa, the tunnel would be about 25 miles (40 km) long and at least 984 feet (300 m) below sea level. If it is built, it will be the world's deepest undersea tunnel.

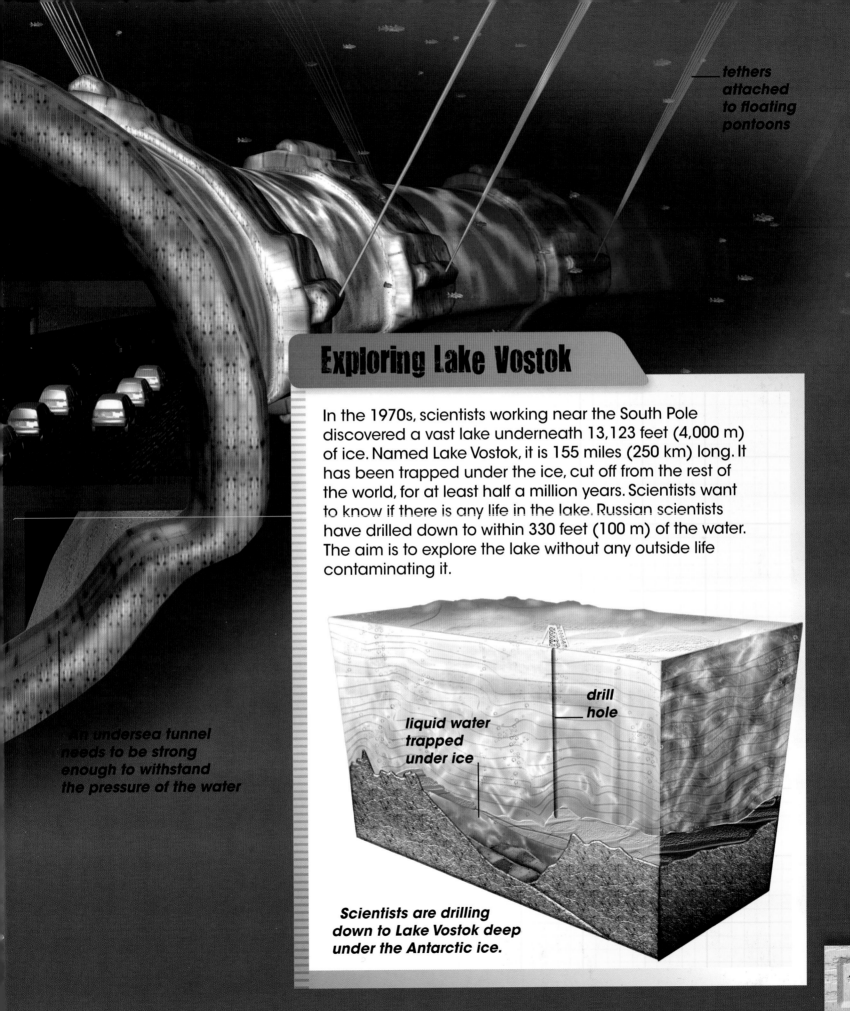

tethers attached to floating pontoons

Exploring Lake Vostok

In the 1970s, scientists working near the South Pole discovered a vast lake underneath 13,123 feet (4,000 m) of ice. Named Lake Vostok, it is 155 miles (250 km) long. It has been trapped under the ice, cut off from the rest of the world, for at least half a million years. Scientists want to know if there is any life in the lake. Russian scientists have drilled down to within 330 feet (100 m) of the water. The aim is to explore the lake without any outside life contaminating it.

An undersea tunnel needs to be strong enough to withstand the pressure of the water

drill hole

liquid water trapped under ice

Scientists are drilling down to Lake Vostok deep under the Antarctic ice.

Glossary

abutment
A massive block of stone or concrete that holds an arch in place.

alloy
A mixture of a metal and one or more other elements. Steel is an alloy of iron and carbon.

amphitheatre
A building, which is usually circular or oval, in which tiers of seats rise from a central open arena.

anchorage
A massive concrete structure that holds a suspension bridge's cables firm.

antenna
The part of a radio that transmits or receives radio signals.

armature
A framework that holds up a sculpture or statue.

bascule
A type of drawbridge that opens upwards, with the weight of the bridge balanced by a large weight called a counterweight.

beam
A long, thick slab of wood, metal or concrete.

bedrock
Solid rock underneath the surface soil.

blow-out
An accidental, uncontrolled eruption of oil or gas from a well.

cantilever
A beam held up at one end only.

canyon
A long, narrow valley with steep sides.

cladding
A building's outer protective covering, usually not load-bearing.

compacted
Compressed or squashed together.

concourse
A wide hallway or corridor, or a large space where several pathways or corridors meet.

concrete
A construction material made of sand, gravel, cement and water. Reinforced concrete is strengthened by added steel mesh or wires.

curtain wall
A type of exterior wall used in the construction of skyscrapers. It hangs from the frame and does not bear any weight.

deck
The part of a bridge that people use to cross the bridge.

decking
Metal sheets that are covered with concrete to make a building's floors.

derrick
A tower on an oil or gas drilling rig, which is equipped with a crane or hoist for lifting sections of drill pipe into position.

dredge
To dig up gravel or silt from under water.

Earth's crust
The outermost layer of the Earth. It is 2 to 44 miles (5–70 km) thick.

earthquake
Shaking and vibration of the Earth's surface caused by movement along a fault.

fjord
A long, narrow stretch of sea between steep valley sides, carved out by a glacier sliding down to the sea.

footpath
The part of a road bridge that is used by pedestrians.

footprint
The area of the ground taken up by a building.

foundation
The lowest part of a structure. The foundations of a building bear the structure's weight and are normally below ground level.

gangue
Worthless unwanted rock mixed with a more valuable mineral.

gantry
A walkway or bridge-like structure, usually high off the ground, that links two buildings.

geologist
A scientist who studies rocks.

geothermal gradient
The rising temperature of the Earth at greater depths.

generator
A machine used to change motion into electricity.

girder
A strong beam, usually made of steel, used in the construction of bridges and other large structures.

grout
Thin mortar used to fill cracks and crevices.

guy
A wire or cable that anchors a radio mast to the ground.

hanger
A vertical cable or chain that links the deck of a suspension bridge to the suspension cables. Hangers are also called suspenders.

hazard
Any risk or danger; something that may cause damage.

hurricane
A tropical storm with winds that blow at more than 75 miles per hour (120 km/h)

hydroelectricity
Electricity that is produced using moving water to drive a turbine. The turbine powers a generator.

ice core
A cylinder of solid ice that is obtained by drilling down into ice.

levee
An embankment or wall built to hold back water.

load-bearing wall
Any wall that bears part of the weight of a building.

masonry
Any structure that is built from bricks, stone blocks or concrete blocks.

mineral
One of more than 4,000 solid chemical substances that form rock.

oil field
An area where oil is found under the ground.

oil well
A hole drilled into the ground to bring up oil from an oil field.

pier
A support that holds up part of a bridge.

pile
A column buried in the ground to hold a building upright.

pilot tunnel
A small tunnel that is bored to test the ground where a tunnel is to be dug.

powerhouse
The part of a dam where electricity is generated.

radio mast
A tall structure, usually made of steel, with radio antennae at the top.

radioactive
Giving out radiation in the form of particles or rays as atoms change from one element to another element. This process is known as radioactive decay and it can be dangerous to humans.

reinforced concrete
Concrete that has steel mesh or wire embedded in it to make it a lot stronger.

reservoir
An artificial lake used for storing water. A reservoir can be created by building a dam across a river.

resonance
The tendency of an object to vibrate more and more violently at certain frequencies.

rivet
An iron or steel pin with a wide head at one end, used to fasten steel girders together.

roadway
The part of a road bridge that is used by vehicles, such as cars, buses and lorries.

rock burst
A sudden explosion of rock flying out of the wall of a very deep mine, caused by the enormous forces acting on the rock deep underground.

service tunnel
A tunnel that lets workers travel to any part of a road or rail tunnel.

solder
An alloy that is used to fuse (join) two metallic parts together.

stadium
A large structure where sports are played, with a playing surface surrounded by thousands of seats for spectators.

stay
One of the rods used to anchor a radio mast to the ground.

strait
A sea channel between two pieces of land.

substructure
The foundations of a tall building, which support it and hold it upright.

superstructure
The part of a tall building that is above the ground.

tier
One of two or more layers, one above the other. Tiered seating is rows of seats, one above another.

tower crane
A large crane, fixed to the ground on a concrete base, which is used to build tall structures.

tremor
A small earthquake.

tuned mass damper
A heavy weight that prevents a building from swaying dangerously by moving in the opposite direction.

tunnel boring machine (TBM)
A giant vehicle with a rotating cutter head at the front that is used to dig a tunnel through the ground. A TBM is often custom-built to bore out a tunnel of a particular size.

tunneling shield
A frame or structure that stops a tunnel's walls and roof collapsing while the tunnel is being dug.

turbine
A shaft or wheel with blades around the edge. When a liquid or gas flows through the blades, the turbine spins like a windmill in the breeze.

ventilation
Replacing stale air or fumes with fresh air.

viaduct
A bridge made from a line of arches or beams sitting on supports.

weld
To join metal or plastic parts together by melting the edges where they meet so that they run together and set as they cool.

Take it further

- Think about the materials used to build skyscrapers and towers. Why do you think these materials are used? Could other materials be used?

- If you were to design your own skyscraper, what shape would it be? Would it be an office block or full of homes? Would it be in a city or in the countryside? Why do you think there are no skyscrapers in the country?

- Is there a river near your home? What sort of bridge would you build across it?

- Why do you think most of the world's longest bridges are suspension bridges? Why are they not arch bridges or beam bridges?

- Think about why the longest bridges and tunnels are built. Would it be cheaper, easier and quicker to build a road over or around a mountain than to build a tunnel?

- Design your own sports stadium. What would it look like? How would you make it look different from other stadiums?

- Most scientists believe that air pollution caused by burning fossil fuels (coal, oil and gas) is changing the world's climate. Clean electricity produced by methods such as hydroelectric plants does not add to this problem. Find out which countries make the most hydroelectricity.

- Think about what the pyramids might have looked like if the Ancient Egyptians had been able to use modern materials such as concrete, steel, plastic and glass. Would they have been a different shape?

- If you could dig or drill a super-deep hole in the ground, where would it be and why would you dig it – to study rock deep underground, to search for gold, or another reason?

- Valuable minerals and oil have been found near the North Pole. Some people would like to drill wells and dig mines to reach them. Others think the risk of accidents are too great and these places should be left alone. What do you think?

Useful websites

www.skyscraper.org
The skyscraper museum has great pictures and information on the tallest buildings. Click on "cool stuff for kids" for further information.

http://skyscraperpage.com/diagrams
Diagrams of the world's tallest buildings – including some not yet built.

www.longest-bridges.com
Log on to see pictures of and find out more about the world's longest bridges.

http://en.structurae.de/structures/stype
Links on bridges, viaducts, tunnels and more.

www.arizona-leisure.com/hoover-dam-building. html
Find out more about the building of the Hoover Dam.

www.london2012.com/webcams/
Watch the video clips to track the progess of the construction of stadiums for the London Olympics.

www.yourdiscovery.com/machines_and_ engineering/tunneltrial/
Dig your own virtual tunnel with this interactive game.

http://encyclopedia.kids.net.au/page/mi/ Mining
A great website all about mining.

Website information is correct at time of going to press. However, the publishers cannot accept liability for any information or links found on third-party websites.

Index